sadi and max Have the Best Christmas in the Entire World

By Brenda Sue

Story by Sadi Belle

Illustrations by Terri Schultz

sadi and max Have the Best Christmas in the Entire World
Copyright © 2023
Brenda Sue

Cover Art by Terri Schultz
Cover Design by Alison Henderson

Published in the United States

ISBN: 9798884507524

Dedication

For Sadi, the most special little human in the entire world.

Acknowledgement

Art, in any form, is the culmination of effort beyond the individual who produces the final product. A supportive family with imagination aplenty encouraged the youngest member to open her mind and embrace her creative nature. As a result, this story has a piece of each person in the family.

About the Authors

Sadi Belle is a dog-loving young lady who attends grade school in Arizona. Practiced in the art of caring for and playing with her puppy and dogs, she loves to weave tales involving them. Her vivid imagination and big heart are evident in the stories she creates for Brenda to write.

Brenda Sue writes in Arizona where she shares a home with her fishing husband and rescue dog, Amigo. She enjoys traveling and spinning tales with her granddaughter. She is an award-winning author of romantic suspense, romance, and cozy mystery under the name Brenda Whiteside.

A Note from the Author

One morning, on the way into town to get donuts, Sadi expounded to me about how special her new puppy was, a blue nose Pit Bull, although he might be a blue Staffy. She also related her knowledge of the bad rap these dogs receive and why. An idea popped, and she was soon bouncing on her seat while chewing her chocolate iced donut. We could write a book about Max and all his wonderful characteristics.

As the months marched on, the idea took shape, expanding and twisting with imaginative tales. This is the first of those stories. I have no idea how many there will be—that depends on Sadi. She's growing up, evolving, and although her passionate love for dogs will never change, the amount of time she'll spend with Nana weaving stories might. We'll see.

Chapter One

Sadi

Sadi didn't care about her bottom being cold. Sitting in front of the Christmas tree, even on the chilly tile floor in her blue nightgown, made her happy. Staring at the decorations on the tree was the best way to start a day. The lights glittered over the green branches and bounced off shiny red and gold balls hanging on the limbs. A few colorful packages crowded together underneath the tree. There would be more presents after Santa came in two days. Her stomach tickled just thinking about Christmas.

Xena snuggled against her left leg, snoring like some old dogs do. Sadi scrubbed her knuckles over the top of Xena's golden-brown head, then rubbed at the loose skin around her neck.

"Aren't the lights pretty?" she whispered to

the dog. She tried to be quiet because Dad always slept in on Saturday, and she didn't want to wake him. But Xena didn't care about the tree or being quiet. She was always quiet. Except for her snore. Which could get pretty loud.

Gabby's white-whiskered snout rested on Sadi's right leg. Gabby sighed and rubbed her white chin against Sadi's leg. The tree lights twinkled in the old girl's eyes. Gabby didn't sleep quite as much as her sister, Xena. Right now, she was content to stare at the tree with Sadi.

Xena snorted.

Sadi giggled. "You're my good old doggie."

Xena's ear twitched, but she didn't lift an eyelid.

Gabby's big, watery eyes looked up at Sadi.

"Yes, I love you too, Gabs, but..." Sadi heaved a gigantic sigh.

Only one thing in the entire world would make this Christmas better. She wished for a puppy under the tree when she woke up

Christmas morning. A wiggly, tiny ball of fur that would run and play and snuggle and play some more. A puppy that was all hers to love. Would Santa bring her one? She sighed. Not much hope. Dad said Santa didn't deal in animals.

Which meant she had to rely on her parents to get her the puppy. But Mom and Dad kept saying she wasn't grown up enough to take care of a puppy. Oh my gosh, she was eight years old! That was plenty grown enough to have a puppy. In fact, she'd be nine in three months, and that was practically ten. Ten was double digit old.

Only two more days until Christmas…

Wait! Maybe it wasn't too late to prove to her parents she could take care of a puppy. She jumped up. Her hand bumped an ornament that flew off the tree. She caught it just before it hit the floor. Whew. Hurrying, she hooked it on a branch. Xena barely opened one eye. Gabby sat with her head tilted to one side wondering what

Sadi was up to.

She darted around the corner and into the kitchen where Mom dipped a tea bag in a cup of hot water. Dad stood by the counter, waiting for his coffee to brew, and scratched his chest. Why was he up so early on a Saturday? He usually slept in at least an hour on the weekend.

"Good morning, Daddy. What are you doing?"

His mouth opened wide in a yawn. "Hmm? Oh, just having coffee."

Weird.

"Would you like some tea, Sadi?" Mom asked.

"Maybe after I feed Xena and Gabby."

"Since when do you feed the dogs?"

"I can, you know. You just always do it sooner." Mom *always* fed the two old ladies. Mom and Dad had Xena and Gabby since before she was born. Sadi loved the girls, but she really wanted a puppy. The old dogs didn't run and play or jump for balls. Mostly, they lay on the sofa and slept. "I'll feed them today." She could prove she was old enough to take care of a puppy.

Mom gave Dad a funny face, like they shared a joke. "Now?" Mom asked Dad.

"Let me wake up." Dad rubbed his eyes. "I need coffee. I may need lots of coffee."

Something was weird with these two this morning, but she didn't have time to figure it out.

Sadi tugged the fridge door open, then stretched her arms up to slide the bowl of doggie stew off the shelf. After breakfast, she'd brush the girls. They'd see she was entirely capable of caring for a puppy.

Mom grabbed the dogs' feeding dishes off the floor.

"I can do it." Her voice squealed, but she had to feed Xena and Gabby without any help.

"Okay." Mom set the dishes back on the floor, then left the kitchen.

"Xena! Gabby! Are you hungry?" She set the dishes on the counter, dragged the step stool against the cabinet, and stepped up.

The dogs plodded into the kitchen. Xena stood beside her, gazing upward, staring at the bowl on the sink. Gabby stopped short, looked at her, then looked toward the doorway. She blinked.

"I'm feeding you today, girl. We don't need Mom. Honest."

Gabby just blinked again as if she wasn't sure if this was good or bad for her.

While Sadi scooped the doggie stew with the silver measuring cup, whispering came from the living room. She paused scooping to listen.

Xena whined deep in her throat.

"Shh, Xena." Why were her parents whispering? Weird. What was up with them today?

Xena shifted from foot to foot and whined again.

"Okay, okay." She finished putting food in the bowls and carried the dishes to the mat, then replaced the stew in the fridge.

"Sadi, when you're done come in here," Mom

called from the living room.

"I'm going to brush them when they're done eating." She raised her voice, hoping she sounded grown up and in control.

"Come in here first." Dad sounded more awake.

Uh-oh. What could they want? She couldn't be in trouble. They hadn't been awake that long. All she'd done was stare at the tree. Well, okay, she knocked off a bulb, but she got it back on. That's no big deal. She put most of them on the tree in the first place. Besides she hardly ever got in trouble.

Heart pounding, she peeked around the corner. Her parents were smiling. That was a good sign. She skipped in and stood between the chairs. "I'm here. What?"

"We've decided to give you one of your Christmas presents early." Mom's smile practically split her face in half.

Sadi glanced around the room. No presents anywhere except under the tree. "You want me to pick one from under the tree?" Opening presents was always fun. Were they rewarding her for feeding the dogs?

"No, no." Dad sipped more coffee, then looked at Mom. "Go ahead. You tell her."

"We're going to go pick out a puppy today. For you!"

"What?" Did she hear right? Her mouth went dry. She could barely swallow. "Like a *real live* puppy?" She croaked the question.

"Of course a real puppy!" Mom clapped her hands.

Sadi jumped up and down. "Yay!" She ran around the chairs and jumped some more. "Yay! Yay!" She grabbed her mom and hugged her tight. "Thank you!" She ran to her dad and hugged him hard, then stared into his face. "I would've fed the dogs a long time ago if I'd known it would get me a puppy."

Dad sputtered his coffee down his shirt, laughing.

"This is going to be the best day ever in the

entire world," Sadi said.

Chapter Two

Max

"My butt's cold," Max whined, then covered his nose with both paws. The only thing colder than his behind was his nose.

"Scooch on over here," Rosie rumbled quietly. "Put your back up against my belly. We'll both stay warmer."

He caught the blanket in his teeth and pulled it with him as he snuggled against his sister. Her brown belly was soft and warm.

"We stayed warmer when Sam and Jake were in here with us. Before they got `dopted."

"You mean adopted." He drew his back paw up and scratched his ear, then rested his head on Rosie's front leg.

"Yeah, that. I wish they'd put those other dogs in with us." She peeked over Max's back and into the playpen next to them where two furry puppies, one black and one white, slept.

"We'd really stay warm if we could all huddle together."

"Nah. Those guys are too bossy, and they'd hog all the toys and blankets. Probably eat our breakfast too." His tummy growled. "Speaking of breakfast, I'm hungry."

"Me too. Is it my `magination, or is it past breakfast time?"

"It's not `magination. It's imagination. And you are right. Man, I hope they don't forget to feed us today." He pushed his head back against Rosie as she licked his ear. "Mmm. That feels good."

"Somebody's got to keep your ears clean, `specially the funny one that won't stand up. Might as well be me."

"It's especially, not `specially. You're funny, Rosie. And you're the best sister a guy could hope for. After we eat, let's play tug-a-war with the rope. What do say, huh, Rosie, what do you say?"

"I `spose."

"It's not `spose. It's suppose. Ouch! What did you bite my ear for?"

His sister giggled. "`Cause you're always correcting me and `cause I can."

"It's because, not `cause. You're hopeless." But he licked her paw anyway, just to show he loved her.

The door creaked, and Max jumped to his feet. "All right! Chow's on, sister."

Rosie whined, her nose sniffing the air. In the playpen next to them, the furry pups yipped and fought each other to stand in the same corner where they knew their dishes would be set.

"Hush you two." Woman carried a tray with four red feeding dishes.

Max liked Woman. She always told him he was cute when she scratched his ears. Her eyes would crinkle, and her teeth would show when she smiled. He'd show her his teeth, and she'd laugh.

Harry stomped in behind her. "Here, Woman. I'll feed the two yippers first." He took two bowls off the tray and set them in the pen for the yippers. "Now for the blue and the female."

Woman followed Harry with the tray and the last two bowls. He set their dishes in a corner of the pen.

"Why does he always call you the blue, Max?" Rosie asked around chewing her food.

"No idea." Max woofed down his breakfast, then waited for his sister to finish. The minute she backed away from her bowl, he licked it top to bottom. *Rats! She ate every last crumb.*

Woman dragged the bowl from under his nose. "You got it all, you hungry little pup." She picked up a jug from the floor and added more to their water bowl. "Have a drink. You too, sister." Then she carried the jug to the yippers playpen and filled their bowl. As usual, they pushed each other back and forth to drink.

"We've got people coming to look at the pups in an hour." Harry stood with his hands on his hips. "What do you think, Woman? Think we'll get rid of the yippers or one of those two first?"

"I don't know about the yippers, Harry, but my guess is the blue will go before the girl, even with his crooked ear. Male pups always go before the females."

"Did you hear that, Rosie?" Max grabbed a chew toy between his teeth and flung it at her. Happy at the thought of getting adopted, he wanted to play.

"Doesn't mean we'll get `dopted." His sister stretched out on the blanket. "`Specially me."

"Not `dopted. Adopted. Not `specially. Especially. But we could."

"You heard Woman. I'm the girl no one wants."

"Ah, she doesn't know. She can't know until the people get here. I bet they'll want both of us." He tackled Rosie, licked her nose, and tugged her ear with his teeth. "We'll get adopted, Rosie. You'll see. This will be the best day ever in the entire world."

Chapter Three

Sadi

"I can't believe it. I can't believe it. I can't believe it!" Sadi bounced in her seat, her voice getting louder with each excited word. Her car seatbelt snapped tight across her chest when she bounced too high. "Oof!"

Mom laughed. "Calm down there, Sadi-lady. You're rockin' the boat!"

"I just can't believe you and Daddy are finally letting me get a puppy. This is the best Christmas of my entire life."

"I hope you remember all of your promises."

Dad's eyes were serious in the rearview mirror, spying on her in the back seat. "A puppy requires a lot of work."

"I promise I'll feed him and walk him and play with him and train him and all the stuff a puppy needs." Sadi gasped with a thought and slapped her hand to her forehead. "What about when I'm not home? I have to go back to school after the holiday. Oh no!"

"How about we share the responsibilities?" Mom craned her neck, peering at her over her shoulder. "When you go back to school after Christmas break, I'll take care of him during the day while you're at school."

"You're the best mom in the entire world."

Dad smiled. "But when you're home—"

"I know. I know." Sadi bounced in her seat again.

Dad stopped their SUV in front of a yellow house. The yard was scratchy looking with dried grass and six cactus plants. One tall, pointy pine stood beside the garage.

"Is this where the puppies are?"

"Yes. These people rescue dogs." Dad turned off the car. "They have four puppies right now waiting for homes."

She pushed the red button on her seatbelt, and before it had time to snap back in place, she flung the door open.

"Wait for us," Mom called.

Sadi danced on the cracked sidewalk, anxious for her parents to catch up. A creak sounded, and the door on the garage crept upward. She froze, holding her breath. The noise was creepy. Mom took her hand and they approached the door, stopping in front as it reached the ceiling.

A smiling lady with short, curly red hair and wearing a green shirt and faded jeans stood in the middle of the cement floor. "Hi. I'm Taila Wagger. You must be the Kirby family. Come on in." She swept her arm through the air like she was showing them the way into a magical castle.

Sadi looked around. It was just a garage with

shelves, a cold cement floor, and two playpens like her baby cousin used. Only these playpens didn't hold human babies. Puppies! Sadi's heart beat fast.

Sadi tugged her sweater beanie down farther over her ears and inched forward, Mom holding her hand and Dad on the other side. Chilly air fluttered on her cheeks. She was glad she wore her sweatpants and long-sleeved T-shirt. Sadi wanted to walk behind Taila Wagger and see the puppies.

"Hey, Woman," a man's voice called from somewhere inside the house. "People are here for the pups."

Taila Wagger turned toward a door at the back of the garage. "I know, Harry."

Sadi pulled on Mom's hand. "Mom, Mom," she whispered. She couldn't wait any longer to see the puppies in the playpens. In one of the enclosures, two furry puppies barked with high-pitched yelps. In the other pen, a brown puppy and a gray puppy peered between the wooden slats.

"Hel-lo-ooo!" A woman called out from the street. "We're here to see the puppies." She scurried up the driveway, followed by a man. They were old, but they moved all peppy and happy.

"Come on in," Taila Wagger said.

Sadi's heart beat even faster. She had to pick out her puppy first. What if they wanted the same one she wanted? When she looked up, her dad winked and nodded. *I think Dad is thinking what I'm thinking.*

The yapping black and white dogs were awfully cute and playful looking but so noisy. Xena and Gabby might not like the noise. And Dad would probably need way too much coffee to deal with them. She let go of Mom's hand and wandered over to the other pen. Glancing over her shoulder, she was happy to see the gray-haired couple reaching into the yappy puppy pen. The man picked up the white puppy, and the woman picked up the black one.

When she got close to the other pen, the gray puppy stuck its nose through the wooden slats. His entire back end was wiggling with his tale wag.

Sadi giggled and knelt. She could feel the cold cement of the garage floor through the knees of her sweatpants.

The brown puppy sat, emitted a quiet whine, and looked at the gray pup. When Sadi put her hand between the slats, the gray puppy licked her fingers over and over. He pushed his face between the slats. Big gray eyes stared right into her eyes. His ears pricked forward, except one of them couldn't point. He had a cute, funny bent ear.

Wow. It's like he knows me. She stared back. "Max," she whispered, "would you like to come home with me?"

She didn't think his tail could wag any faster. He darted at the brown puppy, bumped his head into her, and knocked her over. Then he loped back to Sadi to lick her fingers again.

Sadi giggled.

Mom and Dad stood behind her with Taila Wagger.

"Can I pick him up?" Sadi asked.

"Well, yes." Taila Wagger didn't sound like it was okay, but she said yes.

Sadi cradled Max against her chest. He licked her chin, his chubby little body shivering. "Ah, he's so happy."

"I should tell you, Mr. and Mrs. Kirby, this dog is possibly a pit bull."

"Yes, I can tell," Mom answered. "Although that's a pretty overused term for any dog with his features."

Taila Wagger's eyes went round. "I suppose you're right about that."

Mom knew lots about dogs. "This guy is either an American Pit Bull Terrier or an American Staffordshire Terrier. Hard to tell."

"He was abandoned so we don't know for sure." Mrs. Wagger looked sad.

"Either make wonderful family dogs in spite

of the misinformed reputation that some people wish to repeat." Mom patted his head and got a lick in thanks. "And he's a blue nose."

Sadi studied his face. Hmm. Maybe his grey nose appeared a little blue if she used her imagination. "Can I have him? He's special."

"What makes him special?" Taila Wagger asked.

Sadi stared deep into the puppy's eyes. "I'm not entirely sure yet, but I have a very good feeling about him."

Dad made that sound in his throat, the one he made when Sadi said something he liked.

While Mom and Dad took care of paperwork and paid Taila and Harry Wagger, Sadi sat on a chair with Max in her lap. He was soft and cuddly. He licked her hand, then pointed his nose toward the brown puppy. "Is she your sister?" She stroked his head, and he fell asleep.

Taila Wagger walked them to their car. "You enjoy the blue, Sadi."

"I will for sure. He's my best Christmas

present in the entire world."

A quiet whine came from the cold garage.

"Is the brown puppy his sister?" Sadi stopped walking, hugged her puppy to her chest, and looked back into the garage.

"Yes, she is."

Sadi wished she could take them both home. She peeked at her dad over Max's head.

"Ha!" He said it more than actually laughing. "Don't even think about." He shook his head, smiling, and opened the car doors.

"I hope she gets adopted soon," Sadi told the rescue lady.

On the drive home, Max wiggled in Sadi's lap. He put his paws on the window and watched the world go by.

"Isn't Max so cute? He's silver-grey, I think. I can barely see some tan lines in his coat."

"So you named him Max?" Dad asked.

"No, that's already his name."

"I didn't hear Mrs. Wagger tell us that." Mom looked at Dad.

"She didn't."

"Then, how—"

"I'm not sure how I know, Mom, but I just know. The name came to me when I first saw him."

"He looks like a Max." Dad said. "However he got his name, it fits."

Max

"What's that? Oh, my gosh, what's that?" Max's nose rubbed back and forth against the glass, trying to see everything outside the window as they sped along the road in the car. His wonderful little human, Sadi, held him firm around his middle, and that was a good thing because he couldn't keep his behind from wagging with joy. He probably would've toppled over and ended up on the floor if she hadn't held fast. "This is so fun. Oh how I wish Rosie could see this." He darted a fast lick to Sadi's cheek and quickly returned to all of the wonderful and exciting things outside the window.

"I can feel Max's heart beating a mile a minute against my hand."

"He's one happy puppy," Dad said.

"Oh, Max, wait until you meet Xena and Gabby." Sadi kissed his forehead.

"Oh, yeah." Dad had a funny crooked grin on his face when Max looked back at his humans.

"Who?" Max stared into Sadi's face.

"We'll need to introduce them slowly," Mom warned. "They're old dogs, and it might take time to get them comfortable with a puppy."

"What? Old dogs?" Max bounced around and planted his paws on Sadi's chest. "What's she talking about? Gee, I wish you could understand me, Sadi."

"I think the girls are going to love having a puppy." Sadi kissed his nose. "They can help me take care of him, teach him things."

Dad made a cough-laugh noise that almost

sounded like a bark. Mom fake punched his shoulder. Max knew it was a fake punch because she laughed and Dad made a face. Mom laughed a lot. He liked Mom and Dad almost as much as he liked his little human, Sadi.

Sadi smiled.

He showed his teeth back to her.

"Max is smiling!" Sadi giggled. The sound made Max think of the bubbly noise when Woman poured water into the drinking bowl. He liked that sound. He showed his teeth again just so he could hear Sadi giggle.

"Oh, Max, we're going to have so much fun."

Her happy voice made him wag his tail harder. "Fun, yeah, fun. I want fun."

"I bet Gabby and Xena will treat you like their baby."

"Baby?" Max jumped to his hind feet and put his paws on her chest again. "I'm not a baby!"

"They're old though so I don't think they'll play much." She tickled his ears, smoothing out the bent ear that flapped right back.

He shook his head. "But I'm not a baby."

"I'm the one who'll teach you to play and show you where to eat and where to take a nap and the backyard and my room." Sadi stroked his head. "It'll be fun."

"Fun, yeah, fun. I want fun."

"And you also have to teach him how to behave in the house," Dad said. Dad's voice was serious only not gruff like Harry. Dad sounded like he might laugh if he wasn't careful.

"I know. I'll get him house-trained. You'll see."

"House-trained? Is that part of the fun?" Max licked her chin.

She cuddled him close.

Her arms made him feel safe, and her lap was so warm, nothing like the garage floor or the playpen at Harry and Woman's.

Max forgot about looking out the window or thinking about the old dogs or even about the fun. His eyes got droopy, and he curled into his nap position in her lap. He buried his nose in her sweatpants and slowly, he drifted to sleep.

Chapter Five

Sadi

"Wake up little guy. We're home." Sadi stroked the soft, downy fur between Max's eyes.

The puppy yawned widely and stretched so hard he shivered. He made a smacking noise in his mouth as his lids opened. He blinked. And then as if suddenly remembering where he was, he bolted upright and licked her chin.

"Yeah, we're home." Sadi giggled.

Mom opened her door while Dad strode around the car and to the sidewalk leading to their front door. "Hold onto Max, Sadi, while I unlock the door and greet the girls. See if he needs to do his business. Put him in the grass."

He sniffed around a second, and sure enough, he did.

Sadi scooped him up before he went exploring farther, then followed Mom to the front door.

When Dad opened the door, Xena and Gabby crowded around his legs. "Okay, girls, back up. We have a surprise for you."

Max stirred in her arms. "Just a minute, Max. You'll get to meet your new sisters when we get inside."

Dad herded the girls back into the front entry as she and Mom went through the front door.

Max's wiggling got serious.

Mom laughed.

Xena and Gabby froze when they looked at Sadi and the wiggly puppy. "Whoa, whoa!" Sadi exclaimed. The puppy lurched. It was all she could do to bend her knees to get closer to the floor so he didn't tumble and bump his head.

Max landed on his belly, rolled to the side, and then bounced up on a run. He charged forward. Xena and Gabby shuffled backward. Max scampered forward. Xena shook her head and a low wine vibrated her throat. Gabby's growl and woof sounded far more serious than her sister's. Then, as if they agreed to it, they both turned and ran into the kitchen.

Dad scooped up Max before he could follow.

"Oh my gosh. The girls are afraid of a little bitty puppy." Sadi couldn't help laughing, but she didn't feel bad because Mom giggled too.

Dad held Max, nose to nose, staring into his face. "You little toughie. Are you going to bully the old ladies? You need to slow down and give them time to get to know you."

"Let me have him, Daddy. I'll hold on to him tight this time and stand far enough back that Xena and Gabby can inspect him and get to know him and see he isn't a threat and not growl and just learn to play and—"

"Hold on. Slow down." Dad bent and settled

Max into her arms. "Don't force him on them."

Sadi tightened her arms around Max and walked into the kitchen. The girls sat in the middle of the room, ears up. That was a good sign. Sadi stopped in front of them. "Be still, Max." She thought Max must've understood her because he remained still but snorted and stuck his nose toward them. "He's just a puppy, Xena. Come on, Gabby. He's a sweet guy." She leaned closer.

Xena lifted her nose and sniffed. Gabby shook her head.

"Okay, I'm putting him down."

Max stood at her feet, tongue to the side of his mouth, and then he pounced. The girls ran out of the kitchen, into the living room, and around to the other entry to the kitchen through the dining room. Max was right behind. Around they went four times.

Sadi laughed so hard she had to hold her stomach. Mom and Dad laughed too.

All at once the girls stopped. Max plowed

into the back of Xena and grabbed her tail. Xena made a rumbling noise in her throat and pushed him with her nose. Max dropped her tail and smiled.

Then Max jumped at Gabby who gave a short woof and batted him with her paw. The puppy bounced back and pounced forward then back, forward then back. When he pounced forward the third time, he gave a little yip but didn't get too close to Gabby.

Sadi caught hold of her new puppy and still laughing, she collapsed onto the floor holding him to her chest. "Oh, Max, you are funny." He wiggled so much, she set him down.

And he immediately did his business.

"No!" Mom yelled.

"No!" barked Dad.

"Aghhh," Sadi screeched.

Mom scooped him up and charged for the back door, Sadi running close behind. Outside, she set him on the grass. "Here!"

But Max only ran around in a circle, sniffing the ground, then bouncing this way and that as if the backyard was the best place in the entire world.

Chapter Six

Max

"This is fun. This is fun, fun, fun." Max romped this way and that, loving the feel of grass and dirt and little rocks under his paws. "What was all that fuss in the house? My humans were yelling."

Gabby pranced by him. "You're just a dumb baby."

"I'm not a baby! I don't know everything about humans, that's all."

"We should clue you in about doing your business." Xena pushed him with her nose.

Max took the old dog's push as a friendly touch. "You want to play?" He bounced around the big golden-brown dog. He tried to jump high enough to nip at the loose fur hanging around her neck, but he couldn't reach it.

"Oh no we shouldn't." Gabby leaned her head close to Xena. "Let him learn his lessons the hard way."

That stopped Max from romping. "What lessons? What's a hard way?"

"Ah, come on, Gabby, he's just a baby."

"Why does everyone keep calling me a baby?" No one answered him.

The two old dogs stared at each other. Xena lowered her head. Gabby lifted her nose and planted her paws firmly on the rocks.

Max looked between them. Even though they were sisters, Xena was bigger, and Gabby had more white fur on her nose and neck.

Finally, Xena shook her head and walked back into the house.

Max stepped closer to Gabby, bowed his

head, and stretched his paws out in the grass. His bottom stuck up in the air as he wagged his tail. Maybe if he struck a playful pose, the grouchy one called Gabby would get friendly.

"Grow up, kid." The grump trotted into the house.

"Kid? I'm okay with kid. Better than baby. I'm not a baby." He sniffed the grass, then skittered into the rocks. Suddenly his paws left the ground.

Sadi's soft hands wrapped around his belly. "Come on, Max. I'll show you where your water is."

"I am thirsty."

She carried him into the kitchen and set him next to a giant silver bowl.

As he lapped at the water, Xena nosed in beside him. Max lifted his head, then slapped the water with his paw sending a splash over the other dog's nose. "Funny, yeah?" he asked.

Xena heaved a sigh, a groan deep in her throat, and turned away. "Don't try that with

Gabby."

Sadi giggled.

"At least someone likes fun," Max said.

"Come on, Max." She scooped him into her arms. "I have a ball that's just your size."

"What's a ball?" She sounded happy so he licked her chin. "Is it fun?"

She set him down in the area between the kitchen and living room. From a bin by the wall, she took out a round, red object.

"Oh, yeah, ball. I saw one of those in the other dog's playpen back at Woman's place." That made him think of Rosie. A funny feeling tickled his tummy. He missed his sister.

Sadi rolled the ball, and it bumped his leg. "Get it, Max."

He pounced on the ball, but it rolled away from him when his paw hit it. He charged, and his paw hit it again making it roll farther into the living room and bump into so much color, he couldn't believe his eyes. High above him lights twinkled and sparkly objects filled the air on what looked sort of like the tree Woman had outside the garage.

In front of him, big squares of red and green and blue got his attention. "Fun!" He dove into them, batting with his paw and biting with his teeth. *Fun! Yeah, fun!* A wonderful noise— rrrrrip! He tore harder at the object. Rrrrrip. "Fun! This is fun!"

"Max! No!" Sadi yanked him out of the wonderful objects.

There's that word again—no. He ran around her feet. *Hmmm.* He wanted to have more fun under the tree, but when he dove behind a big red square, Sadi pulled him back and lifted him up.

"No! Those are not for Max. That's a no!"

Max was puzzled, but he was also hurt. "She's yelling at me."

Mom stood nearby. "I'll fix the package. Don't worry."

Sadi touched the red ball to his nose. "This is for Max. Let's play." She carried him away from the color and then set him down. "Let's try this again."

"Okay, but first..."

"Noooo!"

Before he could finish, Mom scooped him up and ran outside. She put him in the same place as before. "This is where you do your business, Max."

Xena ambled over when he finished.

Max sat down. "I sure don't like it when they yell no."

"When they say no, it means you should stop doing whatever it is you're doing. You can do your business *only* outside. Then they won't yell at you. Get it? But don't tell Gabby I told you." Xena turned to go back in the house.

Max chased after her. "What about the other no? Can't we play with those things Mom called packages?"

Xena snorted. "No. Not unless they give you one to play with. Sometimes they let you play with stuff that isn't toys, but you better not do it unless they tell you to. There's always going to be a no, kid. You'll figure it out."

Max didn't have time to think about that because Sadi was there with the red ball. She bounced it in front of him, and he pounced. "Yeah, this is fun."

Chapter Seven

Sadi

Sadi bounced the ball. "Get it, Max."

Her puppy ran but didn't catch up with the ball until it hit the fence and came back at him. He snapped at the ball, but it rolled past him.

Sadi giggled at his antics. She scooped up the ball. Max wiggled, then jumped at her legs. "Let's try it again." This time she rolled the ball.

He gave a tiny bark and chased the ball. This time, he got his mouth around it, then ran in a circle.

"That's a good boy. Bring it here, Max." She

clapped her hands to get his attention. "Come on. Bring it." She held out her hands.

He stopped. Blinked. Then ran at her, but didn't stop. He ran around her legs. When she tried to snatch it from him, he ran away.

"This isn't keep away, Max. I'm trying to teach you to fetch."

"He's probably too young," Dad said from a lawn chair.

"He's got to start sometime."

"Yep, I guess you're right."

The back door opened. "Sadi, bring Max in." Mom was back from the store. "I got him something."

She scooped up Max, and he licked her chin. Mom led them to her bedroom where a wire cage stood in a corner.

"What's that?"

"It's a kennel for Max. This is where he'll sleep at night or stay if we leave the house. He isn't house trained yet so this will be the best way to teach him to be a good puppy in the house."

"But I want Max to sleep with me—not in your room." Sadi knew she whined, but she thought Max could sleep at the foot of her bed. He was her puppy to take care of and cuddle and love. She felt a little sad, and she hung her head.

"He's too young, honey." Mom squatted in front of her and rubbed Max's ears. "He'll need to go out in the middle of the night for a while until he's house trained. You can't take him out in the dark. I'll take him out for you because you need your sleep. You don't want to be sleepy in school." Mom lifted Max from her arms and set him by the kennel.

Max sniffed the kennel, then hopped inside and plopped down on the soft, furry blanket inside.

Mom was right. And he liked the kennel.

Mom kissed her on the cheek and then popped up. "See? He likes it. Look what else I got him." She emptied a sack on the bed.

"Oh! His own collar and leash and food dish.

And, oh! His own Christmas stocking." She hugged her mom. "This is the best Christmas in the entire world. Are these treats for now or for the stocking?"

"Let's put them in his stocking after we hang it up. The girls have treats in their stockings too."

Sadi lifted the leash. "Look at this, Max."

But Max wasn't in the kennel.

"Uh-oh. Where did he go?"

Sadi and Mom tore out of the bedroom and raced down the hallway toward the living room.

"Max! Max!" She worried her puppy was up to something he shouldn't be and would get in trouble. "Max!" But she skidded to a halt when Dad stood in the living room waving one arm in the air while with his other hand, he held fingers to his mouth to shush her.

"Quiet," Dad whispered and pointed at one of the sofas.

Mom and Sadi tiptoed forward and peeked over the sofa arm.

Sadi threw a hand to her mouth to keep from giggling. Xena was stretched out, asleep, and snoring like some old dogs do. Max was cuddled against the old girl's tummy, taking a nap with her.

"Ahhh," Sadi sighed. "Aren't Xena and Max cute?"

Gabby looked at her and then at Max. She

shook her head, climbed into a corner of the other sofa, and lay down with a snort.

"Let's hang Max's stocking while he's asleep," Mom said.

"Good idea." Sadi ran back to her parents' bedroom to get the stocking and treats. "I can't wait for Christmas morning to see the girls and Max get their stockings. This is the best Christmas ever in the entire world."

Chapter Eight

Max

That night, after lots of hugs and kisses from his little human, Sadi, Max settled down in his kennel. Today had been the best day ever in his entire life. He'd learned what no meant. And he'd learned how to make all his humans happy when he whined at the back door to let him out to do his business. Man! You'd think he'd given them the best present in the entire world when he did that. He had two new sisters, and although Gabby wasn't as friendly as Xena, he knew she liked him when she didn't growl at him for licking her food dish. Sadi, with Mom's help, fed them the best dinner ever. His tummy got so full.

Now, the house was quiet. Sadi was in another room, sleeping. Xena slept in Sadi's room on a soft blanket by her bed. He knew Xena's blanket-bed was soft because he'd tried it out...until Xena said, "Beat it, kid." In this room, Mom and Dad were asleep. Gabby slept on her blanket between his kennel and the human bed. Max yawned, curled into a ball, and fell asleep.

Sometime later—Max had no idea what time or how much later—he woke. "What do I do? I need to go out, but everyone is asleep." He stood and walked to the corner of his kennel closest to Gabby. "Psst, Gabby, psst." No answer. He tried again. "Psst, Gabby, psst."

"Leave me alone. I'm sleeping."

"But I need to go out."

"Can't help you, kid."

"Should I just do what I need to do here?"

Gabby was quiet for a long while. Max thought she'd gone back to sleep. Finally, she sighed and raised her head. "Think about it. Think about what to do."

Max paced around the kennel. "Think," he grumbled. "Think." Then he whined and whined and whined.

Finally, Mom spoke. "Okay, Max. I'm coming. Good boy." She opened the door. "I got you. Come on."

When Max was back in his kennel after hugs and kisses from Mom, he went to the corner closest to Gabby. She wouldn't raise her head. She was probably back to sleep.

Max lay down. He thought again about all the things he'd learned today. His humans took care of him with food and play and fun and love. Xena was his helper and cuddler. Gabby was his teacher who made him think. He had the best home in the entire world. He fell asleep.

The next morning, Max was just about to start whining again when his little human tiptoed into the room in her bare feet. She looked funny in a baggy thing that hung past her knees covered in pictures of heads of dogs that looked just like Xena and Gabby. Sadi's hair stuck out in all directions, some of it hanging in her face. The color of her hair, kind of brown and kind of blonde, reminded him of Rosie. She quietly opened his door and lifted him. Her body was so warm and smelled like the fresh blanket Woman would bring them every other day in the garage.

"Come on, Gabby," Max said. "Want to come with us?"

Gabby just snorted and rolled over.

Sadi opened the door to the back yard. "Here you go, Max."

He romped over to the grass, did his business, and then romped around. A flying thing buzzed his nose, and he chased it away. A fat brown bug crossed his path but got under the rocks before he could paw it. The sun peaked over the back fence, and the sky turned a brighter blue. Sadi followed him around, giggling at most everything he did.

After a while, the back door opened again. The old girls plodded outside with Mom.

"Sadi, put these shoes on and this hoodie. It's chilly out here."

"Hi Gabby. Hi Xena." Max ran circles around the dogs.

"You better let us wake up," Xena said. "And I wouldn't bother Gabby until she's had her breakfast if I were you."

Max jumped at Mom's legs.

She laughed. "You silly puppy. Let me get my tea, and I'll come back out. Do you want some tea, Sadi?"

"What's tea?" Max craned his neck up to look at Mom, but she didn't notice. He pawed at Sadi's foot. "What's tea?"

"Sure, Mom, I'll have some tea. With honey. Thanks."

"Honey? Tea? Gee I wish you could understand me, Sadi. I might want some of that stuff."

"Go find your ball, Max." Sadi pointed.

Max saw his red ball lying in the rocks. He pounced on it making it roll. "Fun!" He pounced on the ball again. "Fun! Fun!"

Sadi grabbed the ball and bounced it high. He chased it, clamped his teeth into it, and ran back to her. He dropped it at her feet. "Do it again! Fun!"

"Oh, good boy, Max. You brought it back."

He'd made his little human happy. That made playing with her more fun. She bounced the ball again and again for him to chase until Mom came back carrying what must be tea.

While she and Mom sat at the table drinking from their cups, he followed Xena around, but she wasn't much fun. She sniffed and walked and sniffed and walked. Gabby did the same, but Max decided to not follow her until after she'd had her breakfast.

Chapter Nine

Sadi

Sadi finished her tea. "Mom, are we going to Gram's and Pa's later?" Today was Christmas Eve and the tradition was to visit her grandparents for popcorn and hot chocolate in the late afternoon. Then they would exchange presents which was always so much fun. After it got dark and after lots of goodbye hugs to Gram and Pa, they would drive around and look at Christmas lights on houses. Some people decorated their whole house and yard with lights and moving reindeer and big Santas and little elves and plastic snowmen. Dad always put lights on their house with Sadi's help. They did that last week. Mom made a wreath for the front door. But some of their neighbors did it up big time.

"Yep. Your grandparents are expecting us."

"Can we take Max with us?" Sadi jumped up, knocking her tea cup over, but it was empty and it didn't break.

"No, hon. Better not. He'd get bored."

"Awww." She pushed her cup back. "But he'll get bored here all alone."

"The girls are here, and puppies sleep a lot anyway. He'll be happier in his kennel." Mom knew about dogs, so Sadi really couldn't argue even though she wanted to. Mom stood and picked up their cups. "Hey, do you want to Facetime with Olivia and show her Max?"

"Yay!" Sadi jumped and twirled. "Yay! Yay!

Olivia lived across the street from Sadi, but during the summer and on holidays she had to stay with her father in Alaska. She was her best friend, even though she was two years older.

Olivia would be so happy for Sadi that she got a puppy.

"Come here, Max. I'm going to introduce you to my best friend."

Max bounded across the patio and pounced on her feet.

"Yeah, you good boy. Did you see how he came to me, Mom? I think he already understands what I say." She lifted Max, and he licked her chin. "Yeah, you good boy."

"He is catching on quickly. I think he must be smarter than your average dog."

Sadi opened the door for Mom and closed it behind them. "Yeah. He's no average dog."

"And you're no average daughter." Dad stood at the counter waiting for his coffee. "Happy Christmas Eve, Sadi. How's the new pup?"

"I think he's the smartest dog in the entire world." She walked over to Dad. "Say good morning to Dad, Max."

Dad held out a hand. "Give me a paw, Max. Give me five."

The puppy gave a tiny yelp and slapped Dad's hand. Dad's mouth fell open. Then Max licked his fingers. Dad laughed and looked at Mom. "Did you see that?"

"See?" Sadi squealed. "He's so smart." She ran into the living room. "Come on, Mom. Let's call Olivia." She sat on the sofa with Max in her lap.

Mom brought her phone to the living room, punched the numbers for Olivia in Alaska, and then handed the phone to Sadi before going back to the kitchen.

Olivia's father answered. "Hi, Sadi. I bet you'd like to talk to Olivia."

"Yes, please." Max stretched across her legs, yawned, and fell asleep.

Her best friend's face appeared on the phone. "Hi, Sadi."

"Hi, Olivia. Guess what? I got an early Christmas present and it's a puppy and his name is Max and he's so cute and I wish you could be here to see."

"Oh! Show me. Show me. Put the phone by

him so I can see."

"Oh yeah!" Sadi held the phone down in front of Max's face.

Olivia squealed. "Eeee. He's so cute. Hi, Max. Hi, Max."

"Hey, Max." Sadi bent over him and kissed the top of his head. "Don't you want to wake up and say hi to Olivia."

Max opened an eye, then another eye, and sighed.

"She's my best friend, Max. See her?"

"Max! Max! Woof! Woof!" Olivia said. "Did Sadi break your ear? I like it. Very stylish." She always said goofy, fun things. "Hi, Max, you sweet puppy."

Max poked his nose closer to the phone and licked Olivia's face.

Sadi and Olivia squealed with laughter.

Max popped up and showed his teeth, then licked the phone again.

Sadi laughed so hard she could barely talk. "Oh, stop. I don't think Mom wants a wet phone."

"What?" Mom charged into the living room.

"Max is giving Olivia kisses on the phone." She laughed more.

Mom scooped Max off her lap. "That's nice and a bit cute, but a wet phone isn't good. No more kisses. You talk to Olivia for a few more minutes while I feed Max and the girls. Then come have breakfast." Mom shook her head like she did when she was confused on what to do with what was going on. "Merry Christmas, Olivia," she called as she left the room.

"We'll have to introduce Max to Bratty and Bear. I'm not sure about Luna." Olivia was talking about her dogs. "And not the cats for sure."

Sadi talked to her best friend for ten more minutes, then skipped into the kitchen. Dad sat at the table drinking coffee and checking email on his phone. Mom set plates of scrambled eggs in front of them. Max wandered under the table.

"It's okay right now, but pretty soon you have to teach him to not hang around when we eat," Dad said.

Mom chuckled. "Right now, I want to be sure what he's up to, so he's okay under the table. Puppies can get into trouble very easy."

"Can we take him for a walk after breakfast?" Sadi wanted to try his new leash out. "And can I walk him while you walk the girls?"

"We sure can," Mom said. "Sounds like a good idea."

After breakfast, they put on walking shoes and light hoodies, because the sun shone bright, but the air was cool. Dad and Mom leashed up Xena and Gabby. Max kept biting at the leash when Sadi tried to hook him up. Then he'd twirl around.

"He thinks it's a game," Sadi said. She stamped her foot. "Max!"

"Let me help." Mom held him still while Sadi got the leash hooked on.

They walked around the block. Although Max's legs couldn't take long steps like Xena and Gabby, he could keep up because they were old and slow, and he ran instead of walking. Max jumped and ran and walked and jumped and tumbled. Mom, Dad, and Sadi laughed watching him.

Chapter Ten

Max

Max loved his humans. He loved the grass and the trees and walking around the neighborhood. That's what he heard Dad call it—walking around the neighborhood.

"Fun! This is fun, isn't it, Xena? Isn't it Gabby?"

The girls looked happy, but just kept sniffing the ground as they walked and didn't pay much attention to him. They didn't want to jump or run in circles. Xena tried to chase a butterfly once, but only for a few steps.

When they got back to the street their house was on, Sadi got a big smile on her face and waved at two little humans like her.

"Oh, yay! Leila and Steven."

The two little humans came running over. They looked like fun. Max strained on his leash to jump on them. The one with blonde hair bouncing around her face squealed like he'd heard Sadi squeal when she was happy.

"Oh! You have a new puppy." She bent and tickled his ears and laughed when he licked her.

"Max, this is Leila. And yeah, he's my Christmas present."

"Hi, Leila. Leila! Leila!" He loved having his ears tickled, and he loved when a little human showed him affection. He licked her some more, and she giggled again.

The other little human put his hand in front of Max's nose. "Hey, don't I get to say hi to Max?" He gazed at Max through green-rimmed glasses on a freckled nose.

Max thought he sounded gruff, but he couldn't be sure if he was grumpy or if his voice was just deep for a little human. His freckles made him look friendly, but his deep voice made Max wonder if he was. He decided to hope for the best and licked his hand, then jumped at his legs.

"Of course you can, Steven. See? He's greeting you too."

"Yeah, but you didn't introduce us."

"I'm sorry. Max meet Steven."

Steven bent and smiled and patted his head.

Max thought it would be a good idea to show his teeth to this gruff but friendly friend. That made Sadi and Leila squeal and Max smile bigger.

"We're taking Xena and Gabby in the house, Sadi," Mom said. "If you want to visit for a while, stay in the front yard, and keep Max on his leash."

"Okay, Mom."

Max happily let Sadi lead him over to the soft, green grass. The three little humans sat in the grass, folding their legs in front of them. Sadi let go his leash so he could romp and pounce on them. He jumped from Sadi to Leila to Steven. His little human was taller than these little humans.

He ran behind Steven and pounced on his back. Steven's hair was short on the sides but on the back of his head was a tail the same color as Rosie. Max tried to bite it, but he couldn't reach high enough.

"Hey, you!" Steven's deep voice laughed. "He has a funny bent ear."

"Who you calling funny?" Max jumped onto Steven's legs and grabbed the front of his shirt with his teeth.

Sadi frowned. "But I like it. He's special in a lot of ways. That's just one of them."

Max let go of Steven's shirt. "Yeah, special, not funny."

Leila giggled. "I like it."

He jumped off Steven and plopped onto Leila's lap and licked her. She laughed.

Max thought she laughed almost as much as Mom...but not quite.

"I need to go home," Leila said. "You're so lucky to have a puppy. My two dogs are all grown up."

"Grown up?" Max thought Xena and Gabby were grown up. In fact, they were more than grown up...they were old. Max craned his neck to look up at Sadi's friends. "Sounds like you guys are leaving."

"My pets are all ages, but puppies are the best," Steven agreed. He stood. "See you at school, Sadi. Bye Max."

Sadi lifted Max and then took hold of his paw and jiggled it. "Say goodbye, Max."

He yipped for her. "Goodbye."

Sadi giggled and carried him inside. When they went in the house, the old girls were asleep on the sofas. Sadi got out her pad—that's what Sadi called it when she asked Mom if she could play with it. Max didn't think it looked like anything that would be fun to play. His legs were tired from the walk, and his eyes felt so tired too. In the playroom, Sadi sat on a gigantic, round, soft pillow with her pad, and Max curled up next to her. He fell fast asleep.

Chapter Eleven

Sadi

After Sadi played on her pad for an hour and Max took his nap, she had a busy day with lunch, a bath, and taking Max outside several times. The time finally came to go to her grandparents. She gave Max lots of kisses and hugs before Mom locked him in the kennel. He didn't look unhappy. He snuggled into his blanket. When she said goodbye, he blinked and closed his eyes.

Popcorn, hot chocolate, and the present exchange was so much fun. Gram and Pop got her a soft baby doll that looked real with clothes and a bottle and a tiny crib. They all played a game and laughed and teased each other while they ate popcorn. Dad was the winner of the game one time, and Sadi won one time too.

Then she, Mom, and Dad went Christmas lights viewing. The lights were spectacular, probably the best in the entire world.

At home, after kissing Max goodnight and tucking him into his blanket in the kennel, Mom tucked her into bed. Sadi was so sleepy.

"Goodnight, Mom." She opened her mouth in a gigantic yawn and closed her eyes. "This was the best Christmas Eve in the entire world."

The next morning, Sadi threw back her covers and slipped out of bed. She knelt beside Xena. "Xena, it's Christmas." Sadi ran her fingers through the fur around her dog's head.

The old girl stopped snoring but buried her nose between her paws.

"Okay, you old sleepy head. I'll leave you alone."

She grabbed her robe off the hook on the back of the door and shoved her arms into the sleeves as she tucked her feet into her Crocs. Then she tiptoed into her parents' bedroom. Outside the window, the moon hung low as it slipped out of the sky so the sun could come up. There was just enough light to see Max sit up when she opened his kennel door. Quietly, she lifted him, and glanced at Gabby. The other old lady opened her eyes but bunched herself into a ball as if to say, "leave me alone."

Sadi squinched her lips tight so she wouldn't giggle and wake up Mom and Dad. She wanted to wake them, but she also knew if the sun wasn't up, she should probably wait. She padded down the hall. When she got close to the living room, she put a hand next to her eyes so she couldn't see what Santa had left under the tree, and then ducked into the kitchen. It would be much more fun to wait for Mom and Dad to turn on the tree lights and then see the packages.

"Let's go outside, Max." She opened the door and set him on the patio.

Max ran into the rocks, then sniffed around the grass.

Sadi sat on a chair, but she had a lot of trouble keeping still. The purple sky was just starting to get lighter. The stars faded, and the moon was nowhere to be seen. "Come on, sun. Where are you?" Christmas morning couldn't arrive fast enough.

Max brought her the red ball. She rolled it across the patio. She didn't really want to play. She wanted to open presents. And she wanted to give the dogs their stockings. And she wanted to hear Mom giggle and Dad complain he was getting up too early. It was his thing to do. He got up early every day except maybe one day on the weekend, but he had to tease her on Christmas morning. While she thought about that, the sky got lighter and lighter. "Oh, yay. Oh yay."

Max tilted his head, the red ball sticking out

of his mouth. He made a funny rumbling noise in his throat.

Sadi giggled and took the ball from him. "Oh, okay. You don't know what Christmas is, anyway. You just want to play. Three more times." Sadi tossed the ball three more times, and Max brought it back three more times.

Now the sky could officially be called daytime. She picked up Max. "I want a hug from the best Christmas present in the entire world." She cuddled him close. "You know what, Max? Even if there are no presents under the tree, I'm still having the best Christmas in the entire world of my entire life."

"I'm glad to hear that." Mom stuck her head out the door.

"Yay! You're up."

"I am, but your dad may be in bed a few more minutes."

"Of course," Sadi said.

"Let's turn on the tree lights and have our tea in the living room while we wait for him, okay?"

Sadi sat on the floor, a few feet back from the tree.

Max charged forward and batted a box.

Sadi tugged him back. "No, no, you naughty puppy."

Max charged forward again, batted a box, then turned and showed his teeth.

Sadi giggled and pulled him back again. He loped forward and hit a box, then turned and smiled.

"You think this is a game, don't you? You aren't really going to destroy the packages. What a funny little puppy you are."

They played the game until Mom brought the cups of tea into the living room.

"That's enough, Max."

Max seemed to understand when he crawled into her lap, curled into a ball, and fell asleep.

If Max hadn't been in her lap, Sadi would've had a lot of trouble sitting still and waiting on Dad to get up. Just as she was going to plead with her mom to wake him up, he came strolling into the living room.

"How come no one woke me up?" Dad stretched his arms high, then scratched his chest.

"Daa-dee!" She made big eyes at him. "You're so funny."

He laughed.

"Can we open presents now?"

"As soon as I get some coffee." Dad went to the kitchen.

Sadi rolled her eyes and groaned.

Chapter Twelve

Max

Max totally agreed with Sadi that Christmas morning was the most fun in the entire world. Maybe he wasn't allowed to tear the paper off the packages, but the humans were perfectly happy to let him jump and play in the piles of colors they tossed on the floor. Mom tried to gather it into big bags, but Dad and Sadi stopped her because Max was having so much fun jumping in the papers.

"Come on, Xena and Gabby." Max tried to get the old girls to join in the fun. He romped and jumped and pounced. "Come on, Xena and Gabby."

When Sadi or Mom or Dad threw a new paper down, he attacked it. "Come on!"

"Nah." Xena yawned. "I'm waiting for the treats."

"Treats?" Max plopped down in a pile of paper with only his nose sticking out making Sadi giggle. "What treats?"

"See those stockings hanging above the fireplace? We each have one up there with treats in it. We get special treats every Christmas." Xena scratched her tummy with her hind leg.

Max shoved the paper aside and stared at the stockings. "Do you think I have a stocking up there?"

Gabby harrumphed. "You better, because I'm not sharing mine with you."

Sadi clapped her hands. "Okay, doggies. It's time for your gifts. Xena! Gabby! Max!"

The old girls moved faster than he'd ever seen them move. They even beat Sadi to the fireplace. Their backends wiggled. Gabby whined in her throat. Xena sort of jumped—at least her two front paws came off the ground an inch. Max chuckled.

He didn't know what there was to get so excited about, but if Xena and Gabby thought these treats were worth charging off the sofa for, then he figured he didn't want to be left out.

"Everyone, sit," Sadi commanded.

Xena and Gabby dutifully plopped their bottoms on the floor, but their gaze never left the stockings hanging above their heads.

Max wagged his tail and didn't know how he could possibly sit on his wiggly bottom. This looked so exciting.

"Max?" Sadi made his name sound long. She put her hands on her hips and stared at him. "Sit, Max."

Gabby groaned deep in her throat. "Sit down so we can get our treat."

"Okay. Okay. Treat. Treat." Max did a quick sit, but hopped up as soon as Sadi lifted the stockings from their hooks.

"Here you go, Xena."

Max ran around her trying to see what yummy thing she got.

"Get back, kid," Xena grumbled.

"Here's yours, Gabby."

Gabby shot Max such a look, he didn't even try to see what she got.

"Okay, Max. Settle down. I have a special puppy treat for you." Sadi sat on the floor and put her hand out.

"Wow. Does that smell good." Max jumped around and grabbed the treat from Sadi's fingers. He could barely get his mouth around it. He plopped down on the floor with his little human and chewed and chewed. "This is so good." He chewed some more. "This is the best treat in the entire world."

"That should keep you busy for a while. I've got some toys to play with."

Max didn't care that she left him there alone. He had his two old lady sisters nearby. He'd had so much fun romping through all the colors. And now he had the best treat in the entire world.

Chapter Thirteen

Sadi

"Breakfast is ready," Mom called from the kitchen.

Bacon smells followed Mom's words. Sadi skipped into the dining area next to the kitchen. They didn't always have breakfast together at the table. Sometimes Dad just had coffee, and on school days, Sadi had to eat earlier than everyone else. But on special occasions like Christmas Day, Mom liked to cook a special breakfast that they ate at the table. Together.

"The girls are outside. I'd like you to put Max

in his kennel, Sadi."

"Ah, Mom. He might want to be with us."

"And he might keep you jumping up to check on him. We don't want to worry about him getting into something."

Dad sat at the table. "And we don't need him trampling our toes under the table while we eat."

"But—"

Dad arched an eyebrow which stopped her protest. Whenever Dad arched an eyebrow, she reconsidered her words. His look kind of made her giggle inside, but the look meant he'd made up his mind, and she wouldn't change it even with her best argument.

"We can eat in peace if he's in his kennel," Mom said. "He'll be fine. Give him a chew toy to occupy him."

Mom knew what dogs liked, so she believed her. Sadi went to the living room and scooped up Max, assured him she'd play with him after breakfast, which got her a lick on her chin, and then put him in his kennel.

Breakfast was extra special with spicy hashbrowns, Sadi's favorite, plus bacon and scrambled eggs. Sadi loved Mom's crispy bacon. Mom made biscuits too, which Dad liked way more than she did.

After Dad gave thanks, he passed the plate of eggs to Sadi. "Besides doing nothing today, what's happening?" Once in a while, Dad liked do-nothing days.

"I want to take Susan a plate of the cookies and fudge Sadi and I made," Mom said. Susan was their older neighbor who lived alone next door. "But I thought we might take a walk to the park with the dogs before we do that."

Sadi bounced in her chair. "Oh, yeah. Let's go to the park. Max will love the park. Can we go, can we?"

Dad chewed his bacon, taking an extra-long time chewing slow. Sadi knew he was teasing her by keeping her waiting.

"Mmm, it's an idea. One of many for the day." He took another bite of bacon.

"Daa-dee!" Sadi rolled her eyes. "I tell you what. We'd be very happy if you came along, but we can live with it if you don't." She tried to look serious and not smile to tease Dad.

"What? Go without me? No way are you leaving me home on Christmas Day."

Sadi giggled.

Mom laughed. "Yes, we'll all go to the park."

Well, it was quite a production again getting all three dogs harnessed up and leashes on. Mom had to help Sadi with Max. He darted between Xena's legs which made the old girl grumble. Gabby sat, back very straight, and looked down her white nose, glaring at the puppy. Dad stood off to the side, chuckling at the confusion.

At the park, Sadi wished they could let the dogs off leash, but that was against the park rules. She thought about how much fun it would be to play chase with Max. The old girls would probably just lie down or sniff around like dogs like to do. And Max might run off because he wasn't good at listening yet. So, in the end, Sadi was satisfied running with Max on his leash. The sun was bright, and the day was almost too hot for her sweatpants. But the air was cool and when she ran, her long hair flew behind her.

By the time they got home, all the dogs looked exhausted. Xena and Gabby climbed onto their favorite spots on the sofas. Max could only get his paws up to the cushion. He was too little to climb up. He yipped at Xena. She opened one eye as if to say, "What do you expect me to do?"

Sadi giggled and lifted Max to the sofa.

Max immediately cuddled in against Xena's belly. Xena didn't move, only snored.

"Sadi, wash your hands and then let's put together a plate of cookies and fudge for Susan."

"Mom, can I take Max to meet Susan? She told me once she likes dogs."

"Sure. I bet she'd like that."

Sadi smiled. She wanted everyone she knew

to get to know Max, the best Christmas present in the entire world.

Max

Max stretched and yawned. He stretched so hard he fell off the sofa.

Gabby snorted.

"Not funny." Max's tummy had hit the floor, and his legs sprawled in all directions.

Gabby eyed Max. "Are you okay, kid?"

He didn't get an answer out because Sadi ran to him and scooped him up. "Oh, dear, look at you. Did you fall off?" She cuddled him close.

"Poor me. That helps. Lots of cuddles. Yeah, yeah. I'll be better now."

"Oh, brother." Gabby snorted again, shook her head, and curled into a corner of the sofa.

"Guess what, Max. We're going to go see Susan. She's our neighbor and a very nice lady. You have to be good at her house."

"When am I not good? I'm good. Is she fun? Does her house have fun stuff like our house? Gee, I wish you could understand me, Sadi."

"Let's go." Mom walked past them to the door carrying something that smelled wonderful.

Max sniffed the air, happy that Sadi followed Mom and the good smell. Maybe he could eat some.

They walked along the sidewalk. "She might have company. There's a car parked in front of her house. If she does, we won't stay and visit but just leave the fudge and cookies."

"Leave it?" Max wiggled in Sadi's arms. "Leave the good smell?" Whatever it was had to taste good. "Nah, let's take it back home."

When they got to the next yard, a female

human who was shorter than Mom but taller than Sadi stood in the yard talking to a much taller male human. "How nice to see my neighbors, the Kirbys. Merry Christmas!"

"What a happy face!" Max liked her right away. Her eyes were the same color as the birds called doves. Her hair floated around her face like a white cloud.

"We wanted to bring you some baked goods that Sadi and I made and wish you a merry Christmas." Mom handed the plate of good smells to the neighbor.

"Wait!" Max wiggled. "I'd like to try some."

"This is my son, Claud." The man nodded at Mom and Sadi. "Nice to meet you." But the way he stared at Max made him squirm and hunch closer to Sadi.

"This is Max. He's my Christmas present, the best present in the entire world."

"Oh, look at you, you cute thing." Susan tickled his ear. "You are sweet, Max."

Max licked her hand. She was warm and soft

to his tongue. He looked into her eyes and knew she was a good human through and through. He bared his teeth in a smile.

"Careful, Mother. He may be small, but Max is a pit bull, isn't he?"

"Yep, I'm a pit. I've heard that. Whatever it means, it's me!" But why did the man warn Susan?

"There are quite a few bully breeds," Mom said. "And their bad reputation comes from how the owners handle and treat them. Any dog can go foul if treated badly. Max is either a blue American Pit Bull Terrier or a blue AmStaff. Or a combination. We aren't sure because he's a rescue dog. They make wonderful family pets." Mom patted his head.

"Thanks, Mom." He licked her hand. For some reason she needed to explain all that stuff to this man.

"Okay. Sounds like you know your stuff," the man said.

"Yeah, yeah. She knows her stuff. I'm a great

dog!"

"I've done my research," Mom added.

Research must be good stuff. Everyone looked happy. Max smiled.

"Oh, ho, ho." Susan chuckled. "You're such a sweet puppy. I could love one like you."

"Then maybe you could share those good smelling treats you're holding." Max stared at the plate in her hands. "I'll only eat a little. I'll save you some, promise." He jerked forward, his nose close to the plate of human treats.

"No, no, Max." Sadi clutched him tighter. "Chocolate isn't for doggies, only humans. It can make you sick."

"Sick? That sounds like a bad thing."

"We better get home." Mom gave their neighbor a hug. "We have a Christmas movie to watch."

Sadi gave Susan a hug too while still holding Max. Max rubbed against the nice woman. He didn't know which smelled better, the woman or the treats. He decided the treats because they smelled like food. She smelled like flowers.

On the walk back, he cuddled against Sadi. Above him, the birds chirped in the trees, and Mom and Sadi talked.

"Susan would like a puppy to keep her company, I bet," Sadi said. "She has no one to live with her, and her son hardly ever comes over."

Max perked up his ears.

"She probably would," Mom agreed. "I do feel kind of sorry for her being alone so much."

"Maybe someday we could take her to the Wagger rescue house to pick out a puppy."

"She could adopt Rosie." Max licked Sadi's chin. "Rosie." He pawed her chest.

"I'll put you down when we get home, Max."

"That's not it. Think of Rosie. Ah, gee, I wish you could understand me, Sadi." He slumped against her. If he could only find a way to make her understand.

"I don't know about that, Sadi." Mom shrugged.

"I do." Max cuddled against his little human. "I'll have to think and think about this."

Back home, Sadi set Max on the floor. He ran to Xena and Gabby on the sofa. "Hey, guess where I went. I met a neighbor named Susan and she seemed nice but her son wasn't as nice but he got nice but Mom left the good smelling treats with her and I didn't get any."

"You can't have those treats," Gabby said. "Those are human treats and not good for dogs."

Xena just snored.

"So I don't want to get sick?"

Gabby grumbled deep in her throat. "No, kid, you don't."

A long nap later, Max played with his red ball outside. After that he napped again next to Sadi while she had her lunch and played on her pad. When the sun dropped low in the sky, dinnertime was good as always. Mom made good dinners.

After dinner, everyone gathered on the sofas.

Sadi sat between Gabby and Xena with Max in her lap while Mom and Dad cuddled together on the other sofa. They turned on the television. It made happy sounds and pretty pictures.

"Look at us," Sadi said. "This is the best

family in the entire world. And Max is the best present in the entire world." She kissed his head. "This has been the best Christmas in the entire world."

Max sighed and licked her chin. "I'm the luckiest puppy in the entire world."

Don't miss the next adventure of Sadi and Max in book 2,

Sadi and Max to the Rescue

Yay for spring break! Sadi has a whole week to play with Max, the puppy she got for Christmas. But something is bothering her playful dog. When they bump heads, and Sadi hears a voice, could it be Max, and will anyone believe her?

Max is happy to be part of the family. He loves his humans and the two old dogs that are now his sisters. But he left another sister at the rescue home of Talia Wagger. He knows his sister Rosie is still there and lonely. He has to find a way to get her adopted. If only his little human Sadi could understand him...

A neighbor who needs help and a puppy who needs to be adopted are all part of the adventure in this latest Sadi and Max book. Now that they can understand each other, Max has mischievous plans, but he's also a puppy with a big heart—he enlists his little human on a mission to rescue.

One Further Note from the Author

Encouraged by Sadi, and for this book, I did a great deal of research and reading about the bully dog breeds. These dogs are often identified under the umbrella of pit bull or pitbull, a canine with a bad reputation and not a breed any more than a dog called a mutt. I would encourage you to dig deeper and learn more about the bully breeds. You'll find the following sites very knowledgeable:

World Animal Foundation:

Nanny Dogs: Debunking Myths In The Debate About Pit Bulls https://worldanimalfoundation.org/dogs/nanny-dog/

American Kennel Club:

https://www.akc.org/dog-breeds/american-staffordshire-terrier/

Made in the USA
Columbia, SC
23 April 2024

34428874R00059